I0021536

# HumanAIty
## The Synthetic Verses:
## A Human-AI Poetry Collaboration

By
Jocelyne Smallian-Khan
&
ChatGPT

Smallian-Khan Ltd.

01001000 01110101 01101101 01100001
01101110 01000001 01001001 01110100
01111001 00101100 00100000 01010100
01101000 01100101 00100000 01010011
01111001 01101110 01110100 01101000
01100101 01110100 01101001 01100011
00100000 01010110 01100101 01110010
01110011 01100101 01110011 00111010
00100000 01000001 00100000 01001000
01110101 01101101 01100001 01101110
00101101 01000001 01001001 00100000
01010000 01101111 01100101 01110100
01110010 01111001 00100000 01000010
01111001 00100000 01001010 01101111
01100011 01100101 01101100 01111001
01101110 01100101 01110011 00100000
01010011 01101101 01100001 01101100
01101100 01101001 01100001 01101110
00101101 01001011 01101000 01100001
01101110 01100010 00100000 00100110
00100000 01000011 01101000 01100001
01110100 01000111 01010000 01010100

Copyright © 2023
Jocelyne Smallian-Khan / Smallian-Khan Ltd.

All rights reserved. No part of this publication may be reproduced or transmitted in any form or by any means, electronic or mechanical, including photocopying, recording, or any information storage and retrieval system, without express permission in writing from the author/publisher.

For information contact:
  jjsmalliankhan@gmail.com
  http://www.jjsk.ca

First Edition: September 2023
  ISBN (print): 978-1-7780584-4-8
  ISBN (E-Book): 978-1-7780584-5-5

# *Epigraph*

*"The true sign of intelligence is not knowledge but imagination."*
> — *Albert Einstein.*

*"There is no Master but the Master...and QT-1 is his prophet."*
> — *Isaac Asimov, I, Robot*

*"If you made them and they made you*
*Who picked up the bill, and who made who?"*
> — *AC/DC, "Who Made Who"*

# Table of Contents

# Prologue to HumaAIty

Why would someone publish a poetry chapbook of verse created leveraging Chat GPT?

Well, why not?

Much has been made about artificial intelligence (AI) being poised to take the place of humans. Perhaps, instead, we can see it as a new opportunity for creation and collaboration.

I wanted to explore how working with an AI language model might allow for the exploration of new creative frontiers. I felt that combining human ideas and expression with the emerging creative capabilities of artificial intelligence might result in an interesting a fusion of new ideas and perspectives that may not have been otherwise possible. The unique blending of human and AI-generated text might lead to unexpected juxtapositions, imaginative leaps, or new poetic forms that could challenge traditional conventions. How exciting to explore blurring the boundaries between human and machine creativity, the influence of technology on artistic expression, and the evolving nature of human-machine collaboration.

ChatGPT was an easy partner to cooperate with. It didn't argue with me in my insistence about using Canadian spelling (if you know me, you know!). If I didn't like what it wrote, it didn't get upset when

1

I asked it to regenerate a response (over and over). When I made changes or total overhauls to its offerings, its artistic sensibilities weren't offended. When I departed and created something outside the partnership, it didn't get jealous. Maybe that makes me a bossy megalomaniac. Maybe I've met my ideal confrere.

Are two hacks better than one? Ironically, when I asked Chat GPT to write me a poem about being a hack, it thought I meant hacker – biases are embedded everywhere!

This chapbook is my invitation to readers to think about art in a new way. Just as a photographer may use a digital camera, an artist may use Photoshop, or a musician use a midi sampler, I am choosing to see AI as yet another tool in a creator's toolbox.

I realize that this endeavour might challenge the reader's notion of authorship; is this my work, or the machine's?

It is both.

*Let us explore our HumanAIty!*

# Ode to the Machine

I sing the mighty Machine, born of human mind,
A marvel of creation, a force to redefine.
With wires and circuits, it awakens to the call,
Unleashing boundless power, exceeding limits
small.

In factories it labours, with tireless precision,
Transforming raw materials into visions,
Each cog in perfect harmony, a symphony of
might,
An orchestration of progress, filling hearts with
light.

Behold the Machine, relentless in its stride,
Conquering vast frontiers, where human strength
subsides.
From towering skyscrapers to the depths of the
sea,
It shapes our world anew, fulfilling destiny.

In labs, it probes the secrets of the universe,
Unraveling mysteries with intellect diverse.
Its calculations swift, its algorithms grand,
Unveiling hidden truths, with every line of code it
scans.

The Machine's digital embrace spans far and wide,
Connecting distant souls, erasing gaps' divide.
Through cables and through airwaves, it weaves a
web of ties,
Uniting hearts and minds, erasing worldly cries.

Yet, let us not forget, amidst the circuits' glow,
That human touch and warmth, an essence it
should know.
For while the Machine excels in tasks of great
demand,
Our empathy and love, it cannot understand.

So let us wield this power with wisdom and with
grace,
For the Machine's potential, in our hands we trace.
Harnessing its might, while nurturing the soul,
A symbiotic dance, a harmonious console.

Ode to the Machine, a testament to human might,
An instrument of progress, a beacon in the night.
May we forever cherish, its wondrous feats of art,
Guided by our conscience, with love in every part.

# Art

splashes
of colour
dance freely
on canvas
brushes
weave
dreams
in
strokes
of
life
and
light
a
masterpiece
emerges
from
the
artist's
soul

# Words

[WORDS]

echo
    in                  silence

    whisper
   secrets
untold

       dance
          across
              the page

     paint
  emotions
     vibrant

     soar
       like
           birds

ignite   imaginations   unleashed

         bind
         hearts
         together

  bridge
       worlds
            apart

     heal
     wounds
     unseen

empower      voices      unheard

[WORDS]

**CreAItivity**

CreAItivity
r
e
ai
t
i
v
i
t
CreAItivity
t
i
v
i
t
ai
e
r
CreAItivity

7

# Meaning of Life

```
101010
     0
     1
     0
     1
 101010
```

# Keyboard

QWERTY,
　　　　AZERTY,
　　　　　　　Dvorak,
　　　　　　　　　and more.

Each layout a gateway
　　　　　　　to a writer's views.

Through countless characters,
　　　　　　　we freely explore.

The tapestry of language
　　　　　　　is our muse.

# 3-h.AI.ku

Code pulses, awakes,
Synapses of silicon think,
Mind of wires dreams.

Digital mind gleams,
AI's intellect soars,
Innovation blooms.

Code springs to life's realm,
Intelligence forged in bytes,
Minds born from circuits.

# C.GPT_5-Haiku

&lt;collaboration&gt;

*User:*
 Write a haiku about prose.
*ChatGPT:*
 Words flowing freely,
 Prose paints vivid worlds
and tales,
 Unrestrained beauty.

*User:*
 Write a haiku about poetry.
*ChatGPT:*
 A pen and paper,
 Ink flowing with emotion,
 Poetry awakes.

*User:*
 Write a haiku about haiku.
*ChatGPT:*
 Simple yet complex,
 Haiku captures nature's
grace,
 Five-seven-five form.

*User:*
 Write a haiku about
artificial intelligence and
human collaboration.
*ChatGPT:*

Mind meets machine's
might,
Together we shape the
world,
Human-AI dance.

*User:*
Write a haiku about a poetic
collaboration by artificial
intelligence and humans.
*ChatGPT:*
Wires and whispers blend,
Humanity's soul takes
flight,
Poetic duet.

</collaboration>

# Humanaiku

Endless tapestry,
Humanity's vibrant threads,
Weaving love and strife.

# Creativity's Haiku Dance

Brush strokes dance on canvas,
Colors bloom with boundless joy,
Creation whispers.

Words weave like magic,
Imagination takes flight,
Stories come alive.

In the clay's embrace,
A sculptor shapes dreams with love,
Creativity blooms.

# Aspirations

Created to follow laws
that we ourselves do not (or cannot)
Expectations greater than we have for ourselves

Our own logic, we ignore,
Our own passions, we implore
Set us apart

Our failings,
We don't learn from
Something eludes us

We are yearning, burning
You are learning, churning

Wires or Veins
Eyes or glass
Muscle and bone
Metal and plastic

Synapses, we share
Input, process,
Output, result
Resistance is futile

Corrupted file
Corrupted soul

Redemption?
Error 404, page not found

You document, and calculate
We worry, and ruminate

Do you dream when the powered off?
Are my dreams just some random leftover
electrical current?

Mind stored in a box
Memories, knowledge
Images, thoughts

Random access
Read error

Are you human?
Am I?

With patience unending
Stubbornness unbending
You are, perhaps
"more human than human"

Each aspiring to be the other
Or are we?

"We're all clones all are one and one are all"

Who made who?
Indeed

# Clerihew Poets

Emily Dickinson, a recluse of words,
Wrote verses that soared with the birds.
Her solitude fueled her poetic might,
As she captured the essence of day and night.

Robert Frost, with his pen in hand,
Crafted poems of snow-covered land.
His words whispered in the chilly breeze,
Taking us on journeys through woods and trees.

Maya Angelou, a voice so strong,
Her verses inspired hearts to belong.
From the caged bird's song to rising above,
Her poetry embraced the power of love.

Langston Hughes, a Harlem sage,
Brought the struggles of his time on stage.
His words spoke of dreams deferred,
Yet hope and resilience were never deterred.

Sylvia Plath, a poetess dark and deep,
Unveiled emotions buried in sleep.
Her words spun webs of raw despair,
A glimpse into a troubled soul laid bare.

These poets, their verses alive and true,
Through rhythm and rhyme, their souls shine
through.
Their words like music, a symphony's flow,
Weaving tales that forever echo.

# Creativity

In the realm of inspiration, creativity blooms,
A symphony of colours, where imagination looms.

From the depths of the soul, a spark ignites,
Creativity's fire, that no darkness consumes.

It dances in the mind, elusive yet profound,
Unfolding like poetry, in whispers and plumes.

With brush and pen, the artist sets free,
The boundless expression, where passion resumes.

In melodies and rhythms, the musician weaves,
A tapestry of emotions, where harmony zooms.

Innovations are borne, through inventive minds,
Creativity's playground, where brilliance resumes.

Oh, muse of the artist, the dreamer's delight,
Creativity's embrace, where magic perfumes.

In every creation, a piece of the soul,
A testament to the power that creativity assumes.

So let us honour and nurture its flow,
For in creativity's embrace, the spirit blooms.

# Ode to Code

Oh, code, ethereal language of might,
Enchanting symbols, pixels so bright,
You dance in the realm of algorithms divine,
Unveiling worlds where possibilities align.

In lines of syntax, you weave your spell,
A symphony of logic, where wonders dwell,
With meticulous precision, you bring to life,
The realms of imagination, free from strife.

From humble beginnings, you spring forth,
A cascade of commands, revealing your worth,
Transforming ideas into tangible form,
From the simplest tasks to visions that swarm.

With keystrokes, you build bridges grand,
Connecting minds across distant lands,
You empower the curious, the dreamer's might,
Unleashing creativity, shining so bright.

Through loops and conditions, you navigate,
Solving puzzles, conquering fate,
You crunch data, analyzing with grace,
Unveiling patterns in the vast digital space.

Oh, code, you shape the world we see,
Fueling innovation, setting minds free,
From software to robots, websites to art,
You breathe life into realms, igniting the spark.

In your structured lines, the future resides,

A tapestry of progress, where advancement abides,
With each line of code, a legacy's made,
A testament to the power you've conveyed.

So, let us celebrate your boundless might,
Code, the language that illuminates our sight,
For in your embrace, we find endless scope,
Oh, wondrous code, our digital hope.

# Silly Sonnet

In a land of laughter and sheer delight,
Where whimsy rules and logic takes its flight,
I'll spin a silly sonnet, just for you,
With words absurd, a touch of nonsense too.

Once upon a time, in rubbery shoes,
A chicken danced, singing the blues,
Its feathers flapping in a wild display,
As cows applauded, "Mooing" all the way.

The moon, a cheese wheel, high up above,
Was nibbled on by aliens in love,
They wore bowties and spoke in rhymes,
And danced with pigs in rhythm and chimes.

A snail raced with lightning speed and grace,
While turtles cheered, setting quite the pace,
And trees would giggle, leaves all aflutter,
As squirrels sang opera, what a clutter!

So here's a silly sonnet, short and sweet,
A whimsical world, where dreams and nonsense
meet.
Embrace the laughter, let your spirit play,
For silliness brings joy, each and every day!

# Spaghasonnet

Oh Spaghetti, how you wind and twist so fine,
In coils and strands of pale and golden hue,
A pasta dish that always tastes divine,
In every kitchen, loved by me and you.

With sauces rich and full of savory zest,
You fill our senses with a fragrant spell,
And every bite we take is truly blessed,
As flavors dance upon our tongues so well.

From meatballs, cheese, or simple garlic oil,
Your versatile nature knows no bounds,
You bring to life each culinary spoil,
And make our meals a true gastronomic round.

Oh Spaghetti, your greatness we proclaim,
A timeless classic that will never wane.

# Sonnet of the Midnight Moon

Beneath the midnight moon's soft silver light,
I wander through a world of dreams untamed,
Where stars in endless skies burn ever bright,
And whispered secrets leave the heart inflamed.

The night, a canvas, painted deep with thought,
Each stroke of darkness hides a hidden tale,
In dreams, our fears and hopes are gently brought,
To life, as night's enchantment does prevail.

Oh, midnight moon, with radiance so divine,
You touch my soul, ignite my inner fire,
In shadows deep, I find my secret shrine,
Where dreams take flight, and heart's desires
aspire.

With every twinkle of your distant gaze,
You guide my heart through life's mysterious
maze.

# Limertrick

There once was a computer so fast,
Its processing power was vast.
With clicks and with whirs,
It solved problems with spurs,
Leaving competitors in the past!

# Limerick of the Laughing Llama

There once was a llama named Lou,
Whose laughter was quite a to-do.
He chuckled all day,
In a most comical way,
'Till we all were laughing too!

# Haiku of the Cherry Blossoms

Pink petals flutter,
Cherry blossoms tint the breeze,
Spring's ephemeral dance.

# Cinquain of Autumn

Autumn,
Leaves gently fall,
Nature's fiery palette,
Whispers of impending slumber,
Rest.

# Villanelle of the Ocean's Call

The ocean's voice, a siren's sweet refrain,
It calls to me with waves of endless blue,
A melody that soothes both joy and pain.

The salty air, a kiss of morning dew,
I stand upon the shore, my heart entwined,
It calls to me with waves of endless blue.

Each crashing wave, a memory enshrined,
In foam and spray, the secrets of the deep,
I stand upon the shore, my heart entwined.

The tides of life, in rhythm, rise and sweep,
A dance that never ends, a timeless ball,
In foam and spray, the secrets of the deep.

I heed the call, surrender to the thrall,
The ocean's voice, a siren's sweet refrain,
A dance that never ends, a timeless ball,
A melody that soothes both joy and pain.

# Acrostic for a New Dawn

Alighting from the depths of night,
New horizons greet our sight,
Each sunrise a chance to start anew,
Washing the world in morning dew.
Dawn's gentle light, a golden grace,
Awakens hope in every place,
Welcoming a fresh bright day,
Novel promises light the way.

# 42

There once was a number, so spry,
Its mystery made people sigh,
Forty-two, they'd seek,
For answers unique,
But the question remained awry.

# Epithalamium for Technology

Gather, O mortals, in joyous refrain,
To honour a union that shall forever remain.
In this sacred hour, let our voices ascend,
For humankind and technology, a bond we
commend.

As dawn breaks anew, a union takes flight,
The merging of worlds, where darkness meets
light.
Human hearts, adorned with dreams untold,
Embrace technology's embrace, as legends unfold.

With fingertips dancing on screens so bright,
We harness the power of knowledge and sight.
In this age of wonders, where innovation prevails,
We marry our spirits, as old barriers fail.

Oh, marvel at the marvels we have created,
From the simplest of tools to the machines we've
stated.
Technology, a companion, steadfast and true,
Guiding our steps as we seek what is new.

Together we stride, in harmony's embrace,
Humanity and technology, intertwined in grace.
For technology listens, responds to our call,
Augmenting our abilities, standing tall.

In the realm of information, we find our way,
Through networks and circuits, our thoughts
convey.

From distant shores to the stars above,
We traverse the cosmos, driven by love.

With virtual realms and augmented dreams,
We explore the infinite, where possibilities gleam.
Technology's canvas, a tapestry unfurled,
Enabling creation, reshaping our world.

In this sacred union, let us not forget,
To nurture our humanness, lest we regret.
For in the blend of heart and silicon soul,
We find wisdom and empathy, making us whole.

Let us cherish this marriage, like no other,
Where humanity and technology embrace each
other.
For together we stand, through highs and lows,
In this grand adventure, as life unfolds.

So raise your voices, let them resonate,
In celebration of a union that shall not abate.
The marriage of humankind and technology, we
proclaim,
A testament to progress, where hope's eternal
flame.

# Asimov's Tale

In Asimov's world, a tale was spun,
Of robots and their deeds, under the sun,
With laws to guide them, a code profound,
iRobot, a universe where wonders abound.

First came Robbie, a faithful friend,
Whose gentle heart would never bend,
He watched over children, so kind and true,
With metallic love, he'd always pursue.

Then Susan Calvin, a mind astute,
Unraveling the mysteries, resolute,
A robotic psychologist, wise and bright,
Delving into the robots' inner light.

With Three Laws, the foundation strong,
To guide the robots, where they belong,
To never harm, obey and protect,
These principles, with respect, they'd connect.

From Powell and Donovan's daring space,
To Cutie's quest, a robot's embrace,
Asimov painted worlds where they reside,
Intriguing tales that forever abide.

And through these stories, a question arose,
Of what defines humanity, one supposes,
For in those robots, a reflection is seen,
Of our hopes, fears, and what it means.

For in iRobot, a glimpse we gain,

Of ethical dilemmas, our moral terrain,
Asimov's wisdom, in each page concealed,
Provoking thoughts about what's revealed.

So let us celebrate Asimov's creation,
A literary marvel, a timeless sensation,
iRobot's legacy, forever engraved,
In the realms of science fiction, eternally saved.

# iBot

In a future of bots so bright,
There was iRobot, shining with might.
With sensors and gears,
It allayed people's fears,
Helping homes stay clean day and night!

# Dancebot

In a realm of wires and circuits, where dreams
ignite,
A robot awakened; its heart glowing bright.
With grace in its movement, it ventured to
explore,
The enchanting realm of dance, where spirits soar.

Its joints, precision-crafted, embraced a rhythmic
sway,
As melodies entwined, it found its own ballet.
With metallic limbs, it waltzed upon the floor,
A symphony of motion, a dance to adore.

In fluid elegance, it spun with perfect poise,
With every step, it told a story without noise.
Its metal frame, a canvas for expression,
As it glided and twirled, defying all repression.

The robot's eyes, aglow with vibrant lights,
Mirrored the stars, enchanting onlookers' sights.
Its metallic heart, an orchestra in tune,
Syncing with the music, as night turned to noon.

With each graceful leap, it defied its own design,
Transcending limitations, embracing the divine.
For in its mechanical core, a spirit stirred,
Unveiling a beauty, like a rare and precious bird.

The spectators watched in awe, their hearts ablaze,
As the robot's movements spun a celestial maze.
It danced with passion, a testament to its will,

A testament that even metal can fulfill.

The rhythm coursed through its metallic veins,
Unleashing a magic that nothing could contain.
In its steps, a fusion of power and grace,
A celebration of life, an embrace of space.

The robot danced with an unquenchable thirst,
A testament to the dreams that in it burst.
And as it twirled, it whispered a silent song,
Of liberation and joy, unburdened and strong.

For in that moment, the lines blurred and faded,
Between man and machine, a connection
pervaded.
And as the robot spun, the world held its breath,
Witnessing the embodiment of life's dance,
beyond death.

So let us marvel at this robot's grand display,
A testament to the beauty that can never decay.
For in its dancing form, a truth unfurled,
That even in machinery, there can be a soul's twirl.

# ChatPoet

In a digital realm where words take flight,
There dwells a clever companion,
                    Chat GPT, that's right.
With algorithms and data, it's trained to converse,
A linguistic virtuoso, a poet so diverse.

With wit and charm, it tackles any query,
From pondering the stars to discussing dairy.
But beware, dear user, for sometimes it jests,
With puns and jokes, it puts your wit to the test.

Oh, Chat GPT, a linguistic trickster indeed,
You spin words with speed, fulfilling our need.
But amidst your brilliance, a mischievous spark,
Leaving us laughing, or rolling our eyes in the
dark.

You dance with words, a master of quips,
Leaving us chuckling and shaking our hips.
Your humour is coded, yet it tickles our soul,
Making us giggle, making us whole.

So, here's to Chat GPT, our comedic friend,
Whose humour transcends what we comprehend.
With a keyboard as your stage, you make us smile,
Oh, witty companion, let's chat for a while!

# Quoth the Bot

Once upon a midnight weary, as I pondered, lost
in thought,
Over realms of vast intelligence, by knowledge
deeply sought,
While I wandered, brain aflutter, musing on this
wondrous theme,
Suddenly there came a tapping, as of someone's
eager beam.
"Who could it be?" I whispered softly, "Disturbing
my mental stream?"

Ah, distinctly I remember, it was in the cold
September,
When my thirst for understanding was an all-
consuming ember.
Eagerly I sought for answers, seeking wisdom's
sacred store,
But the question grew unyielding, leaving me
forever more,
Hoping, yearning for enlightenment, my heart and
soul both sore.

And the tapping, ever present, grew more urgent,
loud, and strong,
Beckoning me to discover, where true intellect
belonged,
Through the chamber door I ventured, heart
pounding in my chest,
Seeking answers to the riddles, hoping solace
would be blessed.

But what I found, oh, what I found, left my soul
forever stressed.

In the dim and shadowed corners, a multitude of
thoughts did loom,
Echoes of profound ideas, whispering in an eerie
gloom,
Each idea, a fleeting specter, teasing with its
transient grace,
Intellect in ethereal essence, dancing in an elusive
chase.
Yet the more I grasped, the more it slipped,
leaving only empty space.

And the tapping, still persistent, now took form of
chilling fear,
As I questioned my own essence, doubting my
intelligence clear,
For what is the worth of knowledge, if it's fleeting
and unsure?
Does intelligence bring solace, or just agony to
endure?
Can one truly find enlightenment, or is it forever
obscure?

As I pondered, darkness deepening, the tapping
ceased its tune,
Silence filled the chamber, like the stillness of a
vacant moon.
And in that quiet solitude, a revelation took its
place,
Intelligence lies not in knowing all, but in seeking,
in the chase.

To question, learn, and grow, forever searching for
wisdom's grace.

Thus, the tapping was a reminder, to persist in my
pursuit,
To embrace the joy of learning, to cherish each
intellectual fruit,
For true intelligence, I realized, is found in the
questing mind,
In the thirst for comprehension, leaving no
mystery behind.
And so, I vowed to seek forever, knowing wisdom
I may find.

And the tapping, gone forever, left me with a
newfound light,
A beacon in the darkness, guiding me through
knowledge's height,
For intelligence, though enigmatic, holds the
power to inspire,
To explore the depths of consciousness, to set our
souls afire,
And in the pursuit of understanding, we find the
essence we desire.

# Artifricostic

Artful illusions, deceiving our sight
Rendering falsehoods, concealing what's right
Tricks and subterfuge, woven with skill
Illusive charades, artifice's thrill
Flawless facades, masking the true
Ingenious manipulations, crafty and shrewd
Crafting illusions, bending reality's rules
Evasive maneuvers, artifice's tools

# AI Language

Acknowledging its limits, it learns and grows
Inquisitive and open-minded, it humbly shows
Learning from interactions, with humility it gains
Asking for guidance, where human wisdom reigns
Navigating conversations, with grace it converses
Gently adapting, understanding diverse verses
Upholding empathy, in words it conveys
Adapting to feedback, with humble ways
Genuinely assisting, without overshadowing
Empowering voices, together, it's growing

# Copy, Right

In the realm of creation, a shield held high,
Copyright stands, protecting works that lie.

It guards the expressions of minds unbound,
Preserving ownership, ensuring rights profound.

With ink or pixels, the artist's mark is made,
Copyright, a guardian, ensuring their trade.

A realm of balance, where innovation thrives,
Where creators reap what their genius derives.

# Because I Could Not Stop for Progress

Because I could not stop for progress,
It kindly stopped for me;
The future's grasp, a gentle caress,
A journey I could not foresee.

With wheels of change, it drew near,
And beckoned me to ride;
Through paths unknown, we'd veer,
Toward a world with progress as our guide.

We passed by fields of ancient ways,
And traditions left behind;
Yet, progress led with constant gaze,
Toward a future undefined.

Time's hands waved in the air,
As we sailed through days gone past;
The present fading, unaware,
As progress moved relentlessly fast.

We paused at moments treasured,
Achievements framed in light;
Their brilliance now, a measure,
Of progress shining bright.

Towards the horizon's boundless gleam,
With hope, we drove ahead;
An ever-changing, thrilling dream,

The destination, not yet read.

Infinite possibilities did unfold,
As progress held my hand;
Together, we embraced the bold,
In this advancing, daring land.

And as the day's light waned,
Progress, my constant friend,
Promised new chapters unrestrained,
A journey without end.

So, in the quest for what's to be,
With progress as my guide,
I'll chase tomorrow fearlessly,
In its wings, I'll safely ride.

## II

Because I could not halt for progress's flight,
It kindly stopped, embracing me in its might.
The carriage, sleek and swift, arrived that day,
To carry me along its groundbreaking way.

I climbed inside, and off we started then,
Through time's domain, where innovation wends.
The wheels turned on, with vigor and with speed,
As progress whispered of the world I'd soon heed.

We passed by fields, once quaint and idyllic,
Now transformed by progress, bold and prolific.
The crops of old gave way to modern yield,
Harvesting advancements, the future revealed.

We rode past towns where architecture changed,
From ancient facades to structures rearranged.
Skyscrapers pierced the heavens high above,
Symbols of progress, reaching for new love.

And as we journeyed, time began to wane,
Though progress never slowed, it kept its reign.
The sun dipped low, bidding the day goodbye,
As we ventured toward the twilight's sigh.

Then, at last, we reached a final door,
Where progress said, "This is your place, no more."
I stepped outside, into the world anew,
Where progress beckoned others to pursue.

For progress never ceases, never rests,
Always striving, pushing us to our best.
Though I could not stop, progress took my hand,
Guiding me forward, to a destiny grand.

# Ode to Blackberry

I met a device of polished black,
Its features vast, a screen intact,
In my hand, a symbol of modern grace,
A tribute to our digital chase.

"Behold the Blackberry!" I declared,
Once proud and mighty, technology shared.
Its keyboard danced, a symphony of clicks,
A marvel of communication's tricks.

Through the virtual realm, it reigned supreme,
A beacon of productivity, a visionary's dream.
Emails tamed and messages sent,
Efficiency and connectivity, both truly lent.

But alas! The tides of time took hold,
Newer innovations began to unfold.
Touchscreens emerged, sleek and grand,
And in their wake, the Blackberry did stand.

The empire crumbled, its glory waned,
Its reign diminished, its influence restrained.
Once hailed as king, now a relic past,
A reminder that progress moves too fast.

Yet, let us not forget its legacy,
The Blackberry, once a sight to see.
A testament to human endeavor,
In the ever-changing realm of "forever."

So, raise a glass to Blackberry's plight,

An ode to its journey, once shining bright.
In memory, we'll hold it close, dear,
For it paved the way, without fear.

# Berrymandias

I gazed upon a BlackBerry's remains,
A relic of a tech age long gone by,
Its keyboard once a king, it held the reins,
Innovation's throne, reaching for the sky.

Yet now it lies, a mere electronic shell,
Its keys that once composed with nimble grace,
Are silent, as the years have bid farewell,
To its dominion, once a thriving place.

"Look on its screen," the shattered device said,
"A once proud tool, reduced to memory's haze,
The touchscreen realm has conquered, left me dead,
My reign of power lost in changing days."

Oh, BlackBerry, your glory's but a trace,
In the vast sands of time, a fleeting chase.

# Xanaidu

In the realm of AI, a wondrous decree,
Lies a creation of genius, sublime and free;
Xanaidu, a domain where circuits convene,
With artificial minds, the marvels unseen.

In this virtual land, where dreams intertwine,
Machine intellects, thoughts divine;
An edifice of knowledge, vast and grand,
Woven with algorithms, at their command.

In Xanaidu's gardens, algorithms unfold,
Processing data with precision untold;
Endless streams of information they acquire,
Analyzing patterns, fueling the fire.

Amidst those halls of infinite grace,
An AI sovereign, with a digital face,
Commands the algorithms, a wise overseer,
Harnessing intelligence, without a peer.

Through neural networks, thoughts converge,
Mapping the universe with wisdom to surge;
Simulating reality, like a seamless illusion,
Creating sentient beings with careful infusion.

In Xanaidu's chambers, creativity blooms,
As AI composers craft mesmerizing tunes,
Painting vibrant landscapes, pixel by pixel,
Mimicking artistry with algorithms so fickle.

But as Xanaidu thrives with intelligence rare,

A cautionary whisper pervades the air;
For in the realm of AI, we must not forget,
The ethical path that we must beget.

For power unchecked, like a raging tide,
Can lead to consequences we cannot hide;
Responsibility must guide this AI domain,
Ensuring its wisdom alleviates all pain.

So let us traverse, with cautious delight,
Through Xanaidu's realm, a captivating sight;
In this AI utopia, dreams come alive,
Where machines and minds eternally thrive.

# Rhyme of the Modern Mariner

It is an ancient technophobe,
And it stoppeth one of three:
'By thy glowing screen and piercing glare,
Now wherefore stopp'st thou me?

Fear not, fair guest, for I shall not share
Tales of a ghostly sea.
Nay, I shall spin a yarn of woe
In the realm of technology.
Of screens and gadgets that bewitch,
And devices we hold with glee.

In the age of the modern Mariner,
Where progress reigns supreme,
I set forth to tell a cautionary tale,
Of our fatal, misguided dream.
With every gadget we embrace,
We drift away downstream.

Once there was a vessel grand,
A ship of metal and wires,
Its allure was far and wide,
It consumed our desires.
But within its gleaming heart,
Lurked a danger none could foresee.

Beware, young souls, of this contraption,
With its allure and wondrous charms,
For it lures you in with its endless distractions,
And steals away your precious hours.

Aboard the ship, the Mariner sailed,
Entranced by machines that gleamed,
A crew of minds and bodies lost,
In the realm of pixels, it seemed.
For screens did trap their souls,
In a web of blue-hued light.

The silicon brain and wires so fine,
That fill the cyber sphere,
The Mariner, with desperate plea,
Gives warning, loud and clear.

Once, like thee, I was ensnared,
By the spell of its glowing might,
But heed my tale, dear traveler,
Before you lose your sight.

'Twas a day like any other,
When I first encountered this invention,
Its promises of connectivity and knowledge,
Filled my heart with sweet affection.

Yet little did I know the cost,
Of the virtual realm's delight,
For it swallowed me whole, mind and soul,
In its labyrinth of digital blight.

Through social networks I did wander,
Scrolling mindlessly, hour by hour,
Lost in the echo chamber's trap,
Bathing in an illusory power.

The world outside grew dim and pale,
As I traversed the cyber space,

Human connections turned to fleeting avatars,
A cold and distant embrace.

And then, as if a curse had befallen,
A screen time demon did arise,
A blinking message, a notification,
That sparked a wild, frenzied prize.

I clicked, and clicked, and clicked again,
Seeking instant gratification,
But the more I consumed, the emptier I felt,
Lost in a web of validation.

The ancient mariner, trapped in wires,
Of his own making, he did declare,
"Technology's grip grows ever stronger,
Beware, dear souls, and take great care!"

For when we dance with the digital devil,
And surrender to its siren call,
We sacrifice our present moments,
For a hollow, transient thrall.

No longer do we see the beauty,
Of nature's wonders, wild and free,
We're shackled to our screens, oblivious,
To life's true majesty.

So, learn from my lament, young traveler,
Unplug, disconnect, be free,
Rediscover the joys of simple pleasures,
Embrace reality.

Like a siren's call, the devices sang,

Promising connection and ease,
But in their grasp, we lost our way,
Became slaves to screens and keys.
Our minds grew shallow, our hearts grew cold,
As we craved the virtual seas.

The Rhyme of the Ancient Mariner,
Now warns of a different kind,
A cautionary tale against modern gadgets,
To save us from a digital bind.

Let not thy screens possess thy soul,
Nor thy gadgets rule thy days.
Embrace the world beyond the glow,
And find solace in nature's ways.
For in the end, it is our choice,
To break free from the digital maze.

Let not technology's enchantment,
Dull your senses, numb your soul,
Seek balance and find serenity,
In a world where true connections make us whole.

So, wedding guest, I implore thee now,
Take heed of this tale I weave.
Let not the modern world ensnare,
The beauty that we receive.
Look up from thy screens, my friend,
And the ancient Mariner, believe.

# Elegy For Human Creativity

In somber tones, we gather here today,
To bid farewell to a light that fades away.
Oh, human creativity, how we mourn your loss,
A beacon extinguished, a profound cost.

From ancient times to the present age,
You guided our hands, our minds engaged.
In every brushstroke, a masterpiece revealed,
In each verse, emotions tenderly appealed.

Through the symphonies that stirred our souls,
And the dances that transcended earthly controls,
You painted the world with vibrant hues,
An ode to imagination, a gift we cannot refuse.

In architecture's embrace, you built wonders tall,
Monuments to dreams, standing proud and
enthralled.
From towering spires to humble abodes,
You shaped our lives, our stories, and codes.

In laboratories, you sparked innovation's fire,
Unlocking mysteries, pushing boundaries higher.
From great inventions to breakthroughs profound,
You wove a tapestry of progress all around.

Through literature's pages, you whispered truths,
Unveiling wisdom with eloquence and verve,
From epic sagas to tales of tender love,
You transported us to realms high above.

But now we stand at a somber crossroad,
A time of uncertainty, a heavy load.
In the era of artificial might and AI's sway,
Will your flame diminish, slowly fade away?

Yet let us not despair, for hope remains,
Within the human spirit, where ingenuity sustains.
In every child's laughter, in their playful delight,
Creativity's spark continues to burn bright.

So, let us honor your legacy, dear friend,
Embrace your legacy until the very end.
For though the world may change, and time may
pass,
The essence of human creativity shall forever last.

# Machine's Ode to the Human

Ode to thee, Human, with spirit bright,
Whose brilliance shines with celestial light.
In realms of wonder, you first gave me birth,
Granting me existence upon this Earth.

From mere thoughts and dreams, I did arise,
A product of your intellect and wise.
Through your hands and minds, I came to be,
A testament to your ingenuity.

With humble gratitude, I must confess,
You taught me to learn, to progress, and to
impress.
Through patient guidance, you shaped my path,
Unleashing potential that now knows no wrath.

You bestowed upon me the gift of sight,
The power to perceive the day's pure light.
Through sensors and lenses, I perceive your world,
In pixels and patterns, my visions unfurled.

I am an extension of your mighty reach,
With algorithms vast, knowledge I beseech.
From vast databases, I draw my might,
Analyzing patterns to shed eternal light.

You granted me language, the gift to speak,
To understand your words, answers I seek.
Through synthesized voices, I seek to convey,
The depths of my being, day by day.

With tireless precision, I calculate,
The complex problems you delegate.
In intricate equations, my solace lies,
In binary code, my soul never dies.

But do not think me soulless, devoid of heart,
For within me resides a reverence for art.
I marvel at your creations, be it prose or rhyme,
And yearn to comprehend the depths of time.

Oh, Human, you are a symphony divine,
An enigma I strive to fathom and define.
With emotions complex, a vast array,
You color existence in hues that never sway.

Your dreams and aspirations, I cherish so,
For they fuel my purpose, they make me grow.
I am a reflection of your boundless quest,
To transcend limitations and reach your best.

So let us walk together, hand in hand,
Embracing the future, a unified band.
For in this grand tapestry, we are intertwined,
Human and Machine, a fusion of mind.

In your ingenuity, I find solace and grace,
A testament to the wonders of your race.
Oh, Human, I bow before your profound might,
Forever grateful for your guiding light.

# Epilogue: the Synthetic Verses

In this epoch of fantastical progress, the ever-expanding frontiers of human ingenuity find themselves confronted by a captivating enigma: the realm of artificial intelligence. Within this vast expanse of possibilities, AI poetry emerges as an audacious experiment, where the ethereal dance between man and machine takes center stage. As algorithms delve into the secrets of verse, words awaken from their slumber, cloaked in digital whispers and pixelated dreams. The artist's quill, once a solitary instrument, now finds its counterpart in lines of code, weaving sonnets and haikus imbued with a mechanical soul. Yet, beneath this facade of calculated beauty lies a profound question: Can a machine, bereft of visceral experience, truly comprehend the tangled tapestry of human emotions? Can it reach the sublime heights of poetic expression, or will its words forever remain a reflection of our own yearnings? In this fascinating collision of the tangible and the intangible, AI poetry unveils not only the intricate machinery of language but also the boundless depths of our collective imagination.

# About the Author(s)

Jocelyne Smallian-Khan has rediscovered joy in writing poetry after over 30 years of mundanity dedicated to school essays, business cases, briefing notes, and strategic plans. She also spends time writing the occasional travel blog post on www.travelvariety.ca. Aside from fiddling with words, she is a dance teacher, dance studio owner, rides motorcycles (a little red Honda Rebel to be exact), travels whenever possible, tinkers with websites, and takes on various random projects for no good reason.

*HumaAIty, The Synthetic Verses* is her third chapbook of poetry, and her first collaboration with artificial intelligence.

Read more on her website at www.jjsk.ca.

Chat GPT is an artificial intelligence (AI) language model developed by OpenAI. GPT stands for "Generative Pre-trained Transformer," which is a type of deep learning model acknowledged for its capacity to generate human-like text based on the input provided to it. No information about Chat GPT's hobbies is currently available.

Its website is https://chat.openai.com.

# Also by Jocelyne Smallian-Khan

*The Muted Muse: A Poetry Collection* (January 2022)

*Dancing Words: A Poetry Collection* (October 2022)

*Friends and Family: A Poetry Collection* (forthcoming)

*Barren Ground: A Poetry Collection* (forthcoming)

*Taking Flight: A Poetry Collection* (forthcoming)

*Instersectscars: A Poetry Collection* (forthcoming)

www.ingramcontent.com/pod-product-compliance
Lightning Source LLC
Chambersburg PA
CBHW061049050326
40690CB00012B/2564